How Plastic Changed the World

Stephanie Feldstein

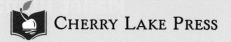
CHERRY LAKE PRESS

Published in the United States of America by Cherry Lake Publishing Group
Ann Arbor, Michigan
www.cherrylakepublishing.com

Reading Adviser: Beth Walker Gambro, MS, Ed., Reading Consultant, Yorkville, IL

Library of Congress Cataloging-in-Publication Data

Names: Feldstein, Stephanie, author.
Title: How plastic changed the world / Written by: Stephanie Feldstein.
Description: Ann Arbor, Michigan : Cherry Lake Publishing, 2024. | Series: Planet human | Audience: Grades 4-6 |
    Summary: "The plastic industry has profoundly impacted our world. The Planet Human series breaks down the
    human impact on the environment over time and around the globe. Each title presents important high-interest
    natural science nonfiction content with global relevance"— Provided by publisher.
Identifiers: LCCN 2023035098 | ISBN 9781668939093 (paperback) | ISBN 9781668938058 (hardcover) |
    ISBN 9781668940433 (ebook) | ISBN 9781668941782 (pdf)
Subjects: LCSH: Plastics industry and trade—Juvenile literature. | Ecology—Juvenile literature.
Classification: LCC HD9661.A2 F45 2024 | DDC 338.4/76684—dc23/eng/20230908
LC record available at https://lccn.loc.gov/2023035098

Cherry Lake Publishing Group would like to acknowledge the work of the Partnership for 21st Century Learning, a Network of Battelle for Kids. Please visit Battelle for Kids online for more information.

Printed in the United States of America

Note from publisher: Websites change regularly, and their future contents are outside of our control. Supervise children when conducting any recommended online searches for extended learning opportunities.

Stephanie Feldstein works at the Center for Biological Diversity. She advocates to protect wildlife and helps people understand how humans impact nature. She lives in the woods in the Pacific Northwest with her rescued dogs and cats. She loves to hike and explore wild places.

CONTENTS

Introduction

Plastic Beach

The Hawaiian Islands are known as a paradise. People love the beaches. So do wild animals. Dozens of kinds of seabirds visit the beaches. Endangered monk seals sunbathe on the shores. Green sea turtles nest in the sand. But a beach at the southeastern end of the Big Island is far from paradise. It's covered with trash.

Ocean currents swirl around Kamilo Beach. They carry garbage from all over the world. It's been piling up for decades. About 96 percent of the trash is plastic. Volunteers try to clean it up. But more keeps coming.

In the 1950s and 1960s, plastic was seen as a great invention. It replaced breakable containers. It didn't leak. It was flexible and strong. It saved people time and money. But it also created lots of waste.

A Giant Industry

Plastic is all around us. It's used in everything from packaging to buildings. But much of it is made just to be thrown away. A million plastic bottles are sold every minute. A trillion plastic bags are used every year.

More than 9 billion tons of plastic have been produced. That's almost enough for every family in the world to have their own dump truck full of it. Most of that plastic still exists. Plastic isn't **biodegradable**. Biodegradable materials break down in the environment. They become part of nature again. But plastic stays in landfills and oceans. It pollutes the environment.

Plastic trash is found all over the world. A giant pool of trash is caught in the currents of the Pacific Ocean. It's called the Great Pacific Garbage Patch. It's twice as big as the state of Texas and is still growing. People around the world are working together on how to stop plastic **pollution**.

Now that waste is found all over the world. It's on beaches and in snow. It's in the ocean and in cities. Bits of it are found in people and in wildlife.

Human **industry** has changed the face of the planet. More than 8 billion people live on Earth. People are living longer. We're healthier than ever. But everything we use or buy comes at a cost. Human industry uses natural resources that wildlife needs. It creates pollution and waste. It can affect human health, too. Our industries put a lot of pressure on nature. The most pressure comes from wealthy countries like the United States.

We need a healthy planet to survive. We need clean air and safe water. We need **ecosystems** with lots of different wildlife. Industries like the plastic industry have a huge impact on the world. But there's a better way. We can change how we make and use materials to protect people and the planet.

CHAPTER 1

The History of Plastic

Plastic didn't exist before 1869. The first plastic was invented to replace ivory. Ivory comes from elephant tusks. People were worried about killing all the elephants. Plastic was created through chemical processes. It could imitate natural materials like ivory. It could be molded into different shapes. It changed the world of manufacturing. People could create whatever they wanted. They didn't have to depend on nature's limits.

The first fully-**synthetic** plastic was made in 1907. Synthetic means not made from natural materials. People spent decades inventing different kinds of plastic. They tested many things this new material could do. But the plastic industry didn't explode until World War II (1939–1945).

Elephant poaching was and is a big problem. In order to get elephant tusks they then trade illegally, poachers kill around 20,000 elephants each year.

Many factories were needed to make materials for the war. The U.S. military used a lot of plastic. Plastic fibers were used for parachutes and ropes. Plexiglass was used for aircraft windows. The plastic factories didn't close when the war ended. They started making plastic for home use. Some factories went from making nylon parachutes to making nylon stockings.

People thought plastic was a wonder material. It was seen as safe and clean. It was less expensive than many other materials. It started to replace natural materials in products and packaging.

Plastic and Human Health

Plastic is made with a lot of **toxic** chemicals. They're part of the process of turning **fossil fuels** into plastic. Plastic releases other chemicals if it's burned. Chemicals can leak from plastic containers. They can get into the products we use. They pollute water and food. They pollute soil and air.

One chemical group is called **PFAS**. PFAS stands for per- and polyfluoroalkyl substances. PFAS can cause chronic illnesses and life-threatening diseases.

PFAS are called "forever chemicals." They don't break down in the environment. They build up in fish and other wildlife. People take them in through food and water. People are taking steps to protect themselves from these chemicals. They're fighting for laws to limit their use. Some companies have already promised to phase out PFAS.

TOXIC

6

About 8 million new pieces of plastic are estimated
to be dumped into the ocean each day.

It's estimated that 100 billion plastic bags are used by Americans each year.

But soon plastic waste started piling up. People started to notice plastic in the ocean in the 1960s. They realized it wasn't biodegradable. Plastic never went away. It kept polluting the environment decades after it was thrown away.

The plastic industry kept growing. Plastic waste tripled between the 1970s and 1990s. Almost half the plastic ever made was created in the last 25 years.

The plastic industry changed as it grew. It started as a way to create products people would use over and over. But now many products are made to be single-use. People use them once and throw them away. Plastic bags, straws, and water bottles are single-use. They're cheap and convenient. But they create much pollution. They harm wildlife and human communities.

MICROPLASTICS

Sunlight and water can break larger pieces of plastic into tiny pieces. These tiny pieces are called **microplastics**. They end up in the air we breathe and the food we eat. They're found in the deepest oceans. They're even found at the top of Mount Everest.

Scientists recently tested the blood of 22 people. Seventeen of the samples had microplastics. That means nearly 80 percent of the people tested had plastic in their bodies. The scientists are worried the pieces can move around the body. But they're not sure yet how this impacts health. More research is being done.

Many restaurants now ask customers if they want plastic cutlery with their take-out orders. Most plastics like these are only meant to be used once.

Many people have switched to reusable containers,
like reusable water bottles, shopping bags, and food
storage containers.

Some businesses even offer discounts to consumers who bring their own reusable containers from home. Many people are making the change to reduce their plastic footprint.

People are even more worried now about the impacts of plastic. They're looking for alternatives. Other industries are creating new materials. These materials are used to make products that can be reused many times.

CHAPTER 2

The Environmental Cost of Plastic

Plastic is an environmental disaster. Most of the plastic ever made is still in the environment. It can take as long as 1,000 years to break down. Until then, it hurts ecosystems.

More than 700 kinds of wild animals are harmed by plastic. Chemicals leak into food and water and make them sick. They mistake pieces of plastic for food. They get tangled in bags and nets.

Much plastic ends up in the oceans. Plastic in the oceans will outweigh all the fish by 2050. More than 1 million sea birds and ocean animals are killed by plastic every year. Plastic trash can make fish, sea turtles, and even whales drown.

Animals can ingest plastic waste, suffocate in it, or become immobilized by it.

There are 825 oil refineries in the world. The United States has a majority of them, at around 130 refineries.

Microplastics are so small they're easily eaten by wildlife. They fill up the animals so they can't eat real food. Microplastics stay in fish who eat them. When other animals eat those fish, they're eating the microplastics, too.

Plastic's impact starts long before it becomes trash. Today, almost all plastic comes from fossil fuels. **Oil refineries** separate oil into different parts. Some parts are used to make fuel. Others make plastic.

Changemaker: Marce Gutiérrez-Graudiņš

Marce Gutiérrez-Graudiņš didn't know protecting the environment could be a career. Then she worked in the fishing industry in college. She met people working to protect the oceans. She wanted to join them.

Gutiérrez-Graudiņš started working to protect coastal areas in California. She noticed no one was involving the Latinx communities. Gutiérrez-Graudiņš thought about where people in her neighborhood would learn about ocean issues. She thought about how people in other communities like hers would learn about them. She thought about how they would get engaged. She held meetings in places that were welcoming to everyone. She translated environmental laws into Spanish. Then everyone in communities like hers could access them.

Gutiérrez-Graudiņš started an organization called Azul. It works with Latinx people to protect the ocean. Azul polled the public about pollution. They found Latinos are more worried about plastic than most other people. Azul helps them address environmental injustices.

Aside from oil spills, another large environmental impact from offshore drilling oil platforms is methane gas. Many oil platforms heat the air around them with methane.

The fossil fuel industry creates lots of pollution. Oil spills kill wildlife. Fossil fuels also cause **climate change**. Climate change makes it harder for wildlife to survive. It **destroys habitat**. It makes it harder to find food. It makes it easier for disease to spread. Climate change harms people, too.

Plastic is poisoning the environment. It's clogging the planet. And there's no way to clean it up. The only way to solve the problem is to stop making so much plastic.

RECYCLING PLASTIC

Most plastic packaging has the recycling symbol on it. But most can't actually be recycled. Thousands of different kinds of plastic are produced. It's expensive to collect and sort. Only 9 percent of all the plastic ever made has been recycled. And it can only be recycled once or twice. Then it starts to fall apart. But glass and metal can be recycled forever.

Turning Off the Tap

Cleaning up all the world's plastic pollution isn't possible. More is made every year. Plastic waste could double in the next decade. Experts say it's like we're standing in an overflowing bathtub. The only way to stop the problem is to turn off the tap.

People are creating ways to replace plastic. Many alternatives are made from plants. Packaging made of cornstarch looks and feels like plastic. Bamboo fabric is replacing plastic fibers. Companies are using nut shells to make jewelry and other products. Palm leaves can be used to make sturdy containers.

But the problem isn't just the material. It's how we use it. Half of all plastic is made to be disposable. It's used once

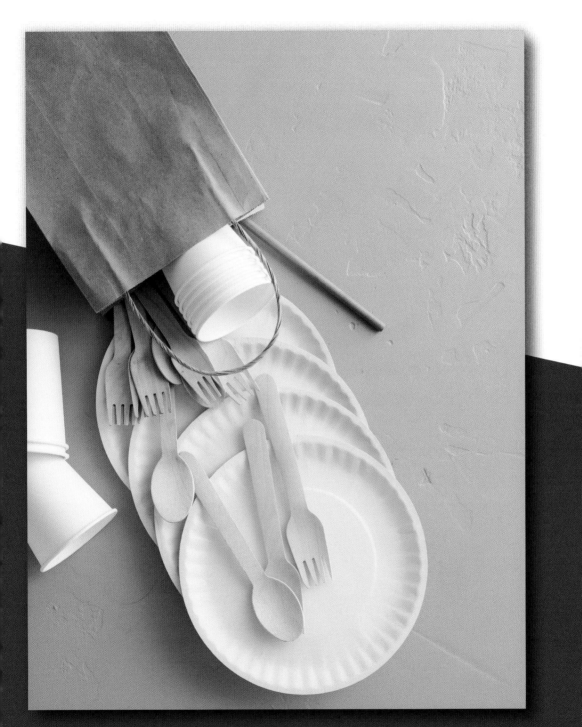

More and more companies are producing eco-friendly alternatives to single-use plastic. Wooden cutlery has a lower environmental impact than plastic cutlery.

In order to "turn off the tap," we need to change how we are buying goods and practice more sustainability.

and thrown away. Also, many products are in plastic packaging. The plastic goes in the trash as soon as it's unwrapped.

Disposable products will always create too much waste. Even less harmful materials come with an environmental cost. Turning off the tap means changing how we use things.

Plastic bag bans encourage people to bring their own bags to stores. Some stores have bulk sections. People can bring jars for foods like nuts and grains. They can buy cleaning supplies in bulk. It reduces plastic packaging.

People are working to change the laws to make reuse easier. People need to be allowed to bring their own jars to stores. Restaurants need easy ways to clean containers. Businesses helping with reuse create new jobs.

U.N. PLASTICS TREATY

Plastic is a global problem. In 2022, the United Nations agreed to create a plastics treaty. It will be the world's first agreement to stop plastic pollution. It will create international laws against plastic. The goal is to cover the full life of plastics. It will look at the dangers of production. It will look at chemicals in plastic. And it will address plastic trash. Leaders are discussing how to reduce the amount of plastic being made. The treaty is supported by thousands of organizations around the world.

The Future of Plastic

Plastic packaging on products like toys is a waste. But some packaging can help prevent waste. Plastic packages help keep food fresh longer. It keeps food healthy. It means less food is thrown away. It saves people money.

Scientists are using technology to design better food packaging. One team came up with a non-toxic wrapper that can be sprayed on food. It's made from an edible fiber. It can be rinsed off when the food is ready to eat. Another team invented "smart" packaging. It's made from parts of corn plants. It can sense when there's bacteria growing. Then it releases tiny organisms. They fight the bacteria and keep the food fresh.

Many of these new materials aren't being used yet. They're still being developed. But researchers are determined to find plastic-free ways to save food.

Many consumers seek out stores that allow them to bring their own reusable shopping bags or refill their own reusable containers.

People are also becoming **conscious consumers**. They're thinking twice about what they buy. They're looking for plastic-free products. They're pushing industries to rethink their packaging. They're creating demand for reusable products.

Activity

What's in Your Trash?

We often don't think about the plastic in our everyday lives. Looking through your trash can help you understand how much plastic you use. It can help you form ideas to use less. Here's how to do it:

1. **Pick a Trash Day.** Plan a day with your parents to go through your household trash. Make sure they don't empty the trash for several days. Set aside recycling, too.

2. **Act normally.** Tell everyone in your family to go about their business until Trash Day. They should throw away whatever they usually do.

3. **Collect the trash.** On Trash Day, collect all the garbage around the house. Keep garbage from different parts of the house separate. Also collect the recycling that's been set aside.

4. **Sort the trash.** Have a tarp or old sheet to protect the floor. Dump out a bag of trash. Sort each trash bag separately. That way you can see how much plastic is being used in different parts of the house. Write down all the plastic you find.

5. **Talk about your trash.** Look at the list of the plastic trash you found. Are there some kinds you can avoid in the future? The goal is to reduce as much plastic use as you can.

Learn More

Books

Beer, Julie. *Kids vs. Plastic.* Washington, DC: National Geographic Kids, 2020.

Feldstein, Stephanie. *Save Ocean Life.* Ann Arbor, MI: Cherry Lake Publishing, 2023.

Salt, Rachel. *The Plastic Problem.* Richmond Hill, ON: Firefly Books, 2019.

On the Web

With an adult, learn more online with these suggested searches.

"7 Facts About Ocean Plastic Pollution for Kids" — kids.earth.org

"Kids vs. Plastic" — National Geographic Kids

"The Story of Stuff" — The Story of Stuff Project

Glossary

biodegradable (biye-oh-dih-GRAY-duh-buhl) capable of being broken down in the environment

climate change (KLIYE-muht CHAYNJ) changes in weather, temperatures, and other natural conditions over time

conscious consumers (KAHN-shuhs kuhn-SOO-muhrz) people who are thoughtful about the impact of what they buy

disposable (dih-SPOH-zuh-buhl) made to be used once and thrown away

ecosystems (EE-koh-sih-stuhmz) places where plants, animals, and the environment rely on each other

fossil fuels (FAH-suhl FYOOLZ) fuels like oil, gas, and coal that come from the remains of plants and animals and are burned for energy

habitat (HAB-uh-tat) the natural home of plants and animals

industry (IN-duh-stree) all the companies that make and sell a kind of product or service

microplastics (miye-kroh-PLAS-tiks) tiny pieces of plastic broken down by sunlight and water

oil refineries (OY-yuhl rih-FIYE-nuh-reez) industrial plants that separate oil into different products like fuel and plastic

PFAS (PEE-fas) a group of toxic "forever chemicals" found in plastic

pollution (puh-LOO-shuhn) harmful materials released into the environment

synthetic (sin-THEH-tik) not made from natural materials

toxic (TAHK-sik) something that is harmful or poisonous

Index